WAY
*Susie*
~~Taylor~~ ~~lor~~

De

by Denise

BOOKS

**Just Us Books, Inc.**
**Orange, New Jersey**

Printed in the U.S.A.
First Edition   10  9  8  7  6  5  4  3  2  1
Library of Congress Catalog Number 94-76810
ISBN 0-940975-50-5  PB     ISBN 0-940975-49-1  HC

**Acknowledgments**
Just Us Books gratefully acknowledges the following publishers for permission to print excerpts from their publications:
    John F. Blair, Publisher. *Before Freedom When I Just Can Remember,* pages 1, 7, 12, and 29.
    Doubleday. *Worth Fighting For,* p. 19.
    Stackpole Books. *In Hospital and Camp: The Civil War Through the Eyes of Its Doctors and Nurses,* p. 25.
    Markus P. Wiener Publishers. *Reminiscences of My Life in Camp,* p. 35.

**Photo Credits**
Photo of Susie King Taylor, page 34, is reproduced from *Reminiscences of My Life in Camp.* Markus P. Wiener Publishers.

# Introduction

I came across the name of Susie King Taylor in 1992. I was preparing a talk on the History of Blacks in Nursing for my sorority, Chi Eta Phi. Other than Mary Eliza Mahoney, I had no knowledge of any Black women who had made their mark in nursing. And, what was worse, the question of Blacks in nursing had never entered my mind. I had taken for granted the accomplishments that my sisters and I had made. Doing research for my presentation changed my perspective on the history of nursing. I realized that I had been told only part of the story. The struggles of Black women in nursing had been omitted.

Like Susie, I made the decision to become a nurse at an early age. I had read about Sue Barton, Cherry Ames, and Florence Nightengale. I dreamed of getting capped and pinned, and caring for the sick. And, like Susie, I saw myself as a nurse during times of war. However, in my daydreams, I pictured myself in an airplane tending wounded soldiers in the skies over Vietnam.

My career never paralleled Susie's career. I attended a very good school of nursing and had no difficulty being admitted. I was never in the military. Instead, I worked in a university hospital where I was readily accepted. And, I took all this for granted. My introduction to Susie set me to exploring the contributions of other Black women in nursing. I now know from whence I came. I no longer take these gifts for granted. I am very much aware of the debt that I owe to this remarkable woman and others.

Why is Susie King Taylor so remarkable?

She's remarkable because of her youth. She was 14 years old and was enslaved when the Civil War broke out. She was 17 and a free woman when it finished. During that short time, she took on several new roles—wife, teacher, nurse.

She's remarkable because she was one of the first Black women to serve as a nurse with the Union Army during the Civil War. She was also one of a very few to write about it.

Susie is remarkable because her story also introduces us to the first Black regiment organized under the Union Army.

She was remarkable because she adds another chapter to the accomplishments of Black women in the history of this country.

The dialogue spoken by Susie and her family in this book is fictionalized. I tried to give a hint of what the speech pattern might have been without straying too far from the speech patterns of today.

—*Denise M. Jordan*
1994

# Contents

*"I was kept at the big house to wait on Miss Polly, to tote her basket of keys and such as that. . . . The day she took me, my mammy cried, 'cause she knew I would never be allowed to live at the cabin with her no more."*
Sarah Debro

# Chapter 1
# A Prayer for Freedom
## 1848–1855

**S**usie sighed as she set the basket on the table in the Grest's bedroom. "Anythin' else, Ma'am?" she asked.

Mrs. Grest sat in a large chair with her feet propped up on a cushion. "Yes, Susie, there is. Run and tell Mammy to fetch me a cool glass of lemonade. I'm feeling parched from all that shopping." Her white skin had pinkened from the heat. Her hair clung to her face in damp ringlets. "Run along, Susie Girl," she added. "And be sure to come right back. I want you to fan me. I'm so hot I feel feverish."

Susie returned quickly from her errand. She picked up the large fan and waved it back and forth. Mrs. Grest sipped at the lemonade Mammy brought, then leaned back, enjoying the breeze Susie created.

*I'm thirsty, too,* thought Susie angrily as she fanned Mrs. Grest. *I'm the one did all the totin' and carryin' whilst we was shoppin'. How come I don't get no lemonade or no fannin'?*

Susie's little brother sat on the Grest bed. He was sorting handkerchiefs. He took his time, first smoothing them out carefully, then folding, then he stacked them neatly. The bedroom door opened and Mr. Grest walked in. He had arrived home early from his business trip.

Mrs. Grest jumped up and gave her husband a warm hug. "I didn't expect you this evening."

"I see," he said glaring at Susie's little brother. "Get that darkie off the bed. I'm all tuckered out and I want to get some sleep."

The boy scrambled down. "Susie," Mrs. Grest instructed, "Help your brother with those things, then make a pallet. You two can sleep on the floor in the corner tonight."

Susie quickly gathered the handerkerchiefs and put them away. Then she got out a pillow and blanket to make a bed. She spread the blanket on the floor and placed the pillow under her head. Her little brother scooted next to her and they settled down to sleep.

Normally, Susie and her brother slept in the slave quarters with their family. Their parents, Hagar and Raymond Baker, were both enslaved and the property of Mr. Grest. According to the law, their children were also enslaved. The Bakers lived and worked on the Grest Farm in Liberty County, Georgia, on the Isle of Wight.

Susie tried to get comfortable. She lay on the hard floor and thought about her parents cuddled in the quarters. She remembered the story mother told about the night Susie was born. That was on August 6, 1848.

"I held you close to my breast and just stared at you," said Hagar. "Yo' skin was the color of the cocoa that Mrs. Grest likes to drink for breakfast. Yo' hair was so thick and curly yo' daddy couldn't keep his hands off it. He kept strokin' yo' hair and touching yo' cheeks. He thought you were the prettiest little thing he'd ever seen. We set for the longest time—just lookin' at you. Then, yo' daddy wished for yo' freedom."

"Hagar," he said, "I pray that somehow the Lord sees fit to let this child be free."

Susie drifted off to sleep. She dreamed of freedom.

In 1855, when Susie was seven, she and her brother moved to Savannah, Georgia to live with their grandmother. Master Grest gave special permission for this move. No trains ran between the Grest Farm and Savannah, so Susie and her brother had to make the long journey by stage coach. The ride to Savannah was bumpy and dusty, but Susie didn't mind.

"Look'a here, Susie!" Her brother tugged on her dress and pointed out the window.

Susie saw people working in the fields or walking along the road. She saw men on horseback and fine ladies in carriages pulled by high-stepping horses.

"Wave," she ordered her brother. They waved and smiled at the people. Often, the people would smile and wave back.

Susie always remembered that ride. The coach driver was particularly marvelous. "His name was Shakespeare and he had a long, long beard that almost reached his knees!" Susie told Grandmother. "It looked as soft as cotton and I itched to touch it." Shakespeare sat on a box with his beard nearly touching his knees, cracking his whip and calling to his horses.

When they reached the city, Susie realized that Savannah was very different from the farming community she'd always known. Houses were closer together. And there were people everywhere!

Susie's grandmother, Dolly Reed, was a free Black woman. No one owned her. She lived on her own and did as she pleased. She still had to have a guardian, but she could own property.

Dolly had a small business in Savannah trading and selling goods. About every three months, she traveled back to the Grest Farm to visit Susie's mother. Along the way, she did some trading.

Susie loved these trips. She looked forward to seeing her family and enjoyed the people she met on the way to the farm. "We gonna' sell apples this time, Grandmother?" she asked. Her cheeks bulged as she bit into the juicy, red fruit.

"Not iffin' you eat'em all before we get there!" Grandmother Dolly replied as she loaded up the wagon with chickens, eggs, molasses, and other things she thought people would want. Then, she helped the children climb onto the wagon seat and off they went—chickens squawking and crates rattling. As the hot sun warmed Susie's skin, Dolly would sing or tell folk tales and stories about being free in Africa.

Grandmother Dolly always stopped at farms and homes on her way to the Grest Farm.

"Miss Dolly's here!" the children from the farms would shout, their arms waving and legs flying. Mothers, with babies in their arms or clinging to their skirts, would come out and look over Grandmother's things. Men in coveralls, skin shiny from sun and sweat, would make their way to Miss Dolly's wagon. They bargained for what they needed, paying cash, or trading bacon, tobacco, or other things.

"Two layin' hens for a side o' bacon," they'd say, or "I'll give this here molasses for some o' them eggs."

While Grandmother was busy, Susie and her brother would play. When Grandmother's business was complete, they climbed back onto the wagon and moved on down the road.

After a nice visit with Susie's family, back to Savannah they'd go. By this time, Susie and her brother would be tired and sleepy. They'd curl up next to each other on the seat, or climb into the back of the wagon. The clip-clop of the horses' hooves and the gentle rhythm of the wagon would lull them to sleep. When they got home, Grandmother would always tuck them into bed.

> *"The white folks did not allow us to have nothing to do with books. You better not be found trying to learn to read. Our marster was harder down on that than anything else."*
> Hannah Crasson

# Chapter 2
# The Secret School
# 1856–1860

I n 1856, it was against the law to teach Black people to read or write.

"You give those Negroes any learnin', next thing you know, they're stirrin' up trouble an' runnin' away," said one slave owner.

"If I find out one o' my slaves can read," said another, "I'll either sell'em or beat'em half to death."

Those that did learn, learned in secret. Those who taught them, taught in secret.

Grandmother Dolly could read and write. "I learned to read so I'd know what was going on," Grandmother Dolly told Susie. "Folks can't cheat me in my business. And," she said, "I can read those newspapers the White folks always passin' around." Dolly wanted her grandchildren to learn, too. So, she sent them to a secret school.

The secret school was held in the kitchen of grandmother's good friend, Mrs. Woodhouse. She was another free Black woman who valued education. More than two dozen children gathered in her house to learn at her secret school.

Grandmother woke Susie and her brother very early on school days. The children scurried around the house, quickly washing and tidying their beds. Then, they gulped down a breakfast of biscuits and molasses, grits, and bacon.

"You children hurry up," Grandmother prodded if they moved too slowly. "And don't be foolin' 'round on the way," she warned as they scooted out the door.

Before they left for school, Susie carefully wrapped their books in paper. No one must ever know that she carried books and was going to school. Then, they skipped down the street— throwing rocks, picking up sticks, and calling to neighbors.

"S-s-susie," whispered her brother. "There's a policeman!"

Susie shifted the package to her left side. She took her little brother's trembling hand in hers and squeezed gently. "Don't you worry none. If he ask, I'll say we makin' a delivery for Grandmother." The policeman looked in their direction, but he paid little attention to the two children.

Susie loved school and learned easily. She continued at Mrs. Woodhouse's secret school for nearly two years. Then, she went to Mrs. Mary Beasley, another friend of her Grandmother's for tutoring. But two years later, in May of 1860, Mrs.

Beasley said to Grandmother, "Dolly, I've taught her all I know. You must find someone else to teach her."

That someone else turned out to be a white playmate of Susie's, Katie O'Conner. Katie lived down the street. While Susie attended a secret school, Katie attended a convent school. After school, Katie and Susie played together and shared secrets. When Katie found out Susie couldn't go to school anymore, Katie made Susie an offer.

"I'll teach you what I learn in school if you promise not to tell my father," said Katie.

" 'Course I'll promise," said Susie. "Your father would skin us alive if he found out!"

So every evening, the girls would get together. Katie would share what she learned. Mr. O'Conner never knew that a secret school was going on in his house.

After four months, Katie entered the convent for good. Susie never saw her again.

Many of the things Susie learned came in handy, especially her writing. In those days, slaves were not allowed to move about freely. They had to show a written pass to travel from one place to another. Even free Blacks, like Grandmother Dolly, were required to have passes. Slaves got passes from their masters; free men got passes from their guardians. And sometimes, the passes were forged.

By the time Susie was twelve, she could, and often did, write passes for her friends and family. Even Grandmother Dolly, whose writing was poor, relied on Susie.

After 9 p.m., the watchmen checked passes, not

every one and not every time. But, a Black person without a pass could be arrested and put in jail. And they stayed in jail until their owner or guardian came to get him or her out. There were times even with a pass, that Black people got into trouble.

"One night, I wrote a pass for Grandmother," Susie wrote in her diary. "She went to a church meetin' on the edge of town. They were singin' this old hymn,

> *'Yes, we shall all be free. Yes, we shall all be free.*
> *Yes, we shall all be free, when the Lord shall appear. . . .'*

A policeman stopped the meeting and arrested everybody there. He said they were planning freedom, singin' "the Lord" in place of "Yankees" to fool anybody who might be listening. Grandmother was spittin' fire! She sent to her guardian right away, so she didn't have to spend the night in jail like some of the others."

Susie didn't have to worry about passes for much longer. Her life was about to be changed by the very Yankees Grandmother was accused of singing about.

> *"There is a war commenced between the North and the South. If the North whups, you will be as free a man as I is. If the South whups, you will be a slave all your days."*
> Ben Walton, as told by Hannah Crasson

## Chapter 3
# Escape to the Islands
## 1860–1862

**B**y 1860, people in this country were arguing over slavery and the right of each state to make its own decisions. Abraham Lincoln and his Union followers in the North believed that in some states, slavery should not be allowed. He also believed that once a state was a part of the Union, it stayed a part of the Union.

Many Southern leaders disagreed. "You can't tell us what to do with our slaves," they argued.

"We need our slaves to work the land," said Southern plantation owners. These Southerners threatened to break away from the United States and set up their own government.

"You try to leave the Union, we'll stop you!" threatened Lincoln.

"You try to stop us, and you'll have a fight on your hands!" answered Southern leaders.

February 1861, leaders in the Southern States formed a separate government they called the Confederate States of America. President Lincoln ordered the Union Army to get ready to march. The South was in rebellion, and the North was going to put a stop to it.

The Civil War started in South Carolina. Georgia was soon caught up in the struggle. In April, 1862, Fort Pulaski, which guarded Savannah's coast line, was attacked and taken by Union soldiers.

The fighting was terrifying. All around Susie, the city of Savannah was rocked by cannon balls and musket fire. The ground trembled and houses shook; glass shattered in windows. Flames leapt as houses burned. Men shouted. Mothers screamed. Children cried. People were dying.

Grandmother, Susie, and her brother ran for cover. Everywhere they went, people talked about the war.

"We'll whip those Yankees in no time," some of the white folks boasted. "Those Northerners won't last long."

But some of the Black folks whispered, "The Yankees will set us free."

Grandmother Dolly, too, believed the Yankees meant freedom. But she was worried about the children's safety until freedom came. Tearfully, she sent them back to the Grest Farm.

The Grest Farm was not as quiet as Grandmother thought. News of the capture of Fort Pulaski had already reached Liberty County. Slave owners were afraid Yankee soldiers were on the way.

"The Yankees will steal us blind," said Mr. Grest angrily. "They'll take our slaves and steal our horses."

"I'm worried they'll burn my farm," said Mr. Smith. He owned a nearby plantation.

"I got my family to think about," said another plantation owner. Some of the slave owners packed up and left; some of them hired extra guards.

Meanwhile, slaves spoke of freedom. "Big Sam over on Ol' Man Smith's place done took off," Susie's cousin told her. "He took his whole family."

Susie's uncle explained, "Heard if you got to St. Catherine's Island, the Yankees won't let the slave catchers get you." Then in a low voice he said, "Me and yo' father been thinkin' 'bout makin' a run for it."

Secretly, Susie's family gathered food, clothing, and a few precious belongings. On the night of the escape, Susie poked her head out of the cabin door and peered into the dark. "Come on," she urged.

"Careful," whispered Susie's mother as one of the children stumbled.

"Quiet," warned Susie's father. With hearts racing, hands sweaty, the Baker family crept toward the harbor.

Susie's uncle, his wife and children, and several other families were already there, waiting. Silently, they boarded boats.

"Get in with us, Susie," said her aunt. "I need your help with the babies." Susie climbed in. By the light of the moon, the small fleet of boats set sail for freedom.

They hadn't gone far when they were spotted by Southern Rebel gunboats. Suddenly, bullets whacked into the side of the boats as the Rebels opened fire.

"Oh Lord, help us," sobbed Susie's aunt. The men struggled with the boats, trying to steer clear of the bullets.

One boat sank and the rebels cheered. Another boat was damaged by gunfire and had to turn back. Only one boat reached St. Catherine's Island—Susie's boat. Her parents, her brothers, and her sisters were lost. Susie wrapped her arms around her aunt's waist and cried.

The group of refugees stayed on St. Catherine's Island for two weeks. Then, Yankee gunboats transported them to St. Simon. This was a larger island a few miles away. On the way to St. Simon, the ship's captain noticed Susie. Though she was only fourteen, her grown-up manner and proper speech intrigued him.

One day the captain asked, "Can you read?"

"Yes, Suh," Susie answered, smiling widely.

The captain was surprised. "Can you write, too?"

"Yes, Suh. I can do that, too," Susie replied proudly.

The captain handed Susie a book and a pencil and asked her to write her name and where she was from. Grinning, Susie took the pencil and wrote, Susie Baker, Savannah, Georgia in big, bold, letters.

"You seem so different from the other Colored people," said the captain.

Susie corrected him. "No, Suh. The only

difference is they was raised in the country, and I was raised in the city. I had the chance to go to school. They did not!"

"Well," laughed the captain, "you certainly are a smart young lady. Maybe we can use your help."

> *"If there was one thing
> the Negro had yearned for in his days
> of slavery, it was education."*
> Mc Carthy and Reddick

# Chapter 4
# Susie the Teacher
## 1862–1863

S usie missed her family, but she kept busy helping with the children, the cooking, and wherever she was needed. On the third day at St. Simon's Island, one of the camp commanders called for her. Susie was very nervous. What could he want?

Susie Baker stood bravely before Commodore Goldsborough. Finally, he spoke. "The ship's captain told me about you." Susie waited. Commodore Goldsborough's eyes narrowed. "How would you like to be in charge of a school for the Black children on the island?"

Susie's eyes widened like saucers. "Me, Suh? Be in charge . . . of a school!"

The Yankee commander laughed. "Think you could teach these children how to read and write?"

"Oh yes, Suh." Susie clasped her hands in front

of her and spun around in a circle. "I surely can, Suh." She stopped spinning. "But . . ." she added quickly, "I'll need some books." She hesitated, then added, "And supplies."

Commodore Goldsborough rubbed his chin and pursed his lips. "It'll take some time, but you shall have them."

Two weeks later, Susie received two large boxes. Her hands trembled as she ripped open the cartons. Inside, were books: Bibles, primers, copybooks—books that did not have to be wrapped in paper and hidden from view. She pulled out an expensive looking book and ran her hands over the soft leather cover. Carefully, she turned the pages and stared at the colorful illustrations. She hugged the book to her chest. Susie, only fourteen years old, was going to be a teacher!

Susie taught school in an old cabin with only a few tables and chairs. Most of the children had to sit on the floor. She held up a slate board and wrote the alphabet in large letters.

"A-B-C," said Susie.

"A-B-C," the class recited.

Then, Susie helped her students with writing.

"Hold the pencil like this," Susie said. She bent down and helped to guide their awkward fingers. She praised each success and scolded those whom she thought weren't trying their best.

The children weren't the only ones who wanted to learn how to read and write. Their parents hadn't been allowed to learn while they were enslaved and they were hungry for knowledge. So—in the evening, after the work was done and the children were down for the night—Susie taught them, too.

When the war first started, Black men were not allowed to be soldiers. They volunteered to fight for the Union Army. They were told, "No Negro soldiers wanted."

Some free Black men from Philadelphia, Detroit, and Chicago offered a different kind of help. "We'll go into the South and band the slaves together. We'll make armies of them." Lincoln and his followers still refused their help. "We don't need Negro armies," they said.

However, the war lasted much longer than anyone thought possible. Thousands of lives had already been lost and no one could predict when the war would end. More men were needed.

President Lincoln soon changed his mind. Two years after the start of the war, he announced, "January 1, 1z863, slaves in the Confederate States will be free." With this announcement came the right and the duty for Black men to fight for freedom.

Men from St. Simon's Island were chosen to fill out a regiment of Black soldiers. They were called the 1st South Carolina Volunteers. The name was later changed to the 33d United States Colored Troops.

One of these Black soldiers was Sergeant Edward King from Company E. Like Susie, he could read and write. When Sergeant King was off duty, he would work with Susie. Together, they would teach reading and writing to the adults. Now and then, Sergeant King's eyes would stray from his book to Susie.

Sometimes, when they were through teaching, he'd say, "We're done for the night, Miss Susie. Can I escort you to your cabin?"

Sometimes, he surprised her with flowers. "These are for you, Miss Susie." Susie would bury her nose in the sweet blossoms.

Susie liked him—a lot. One day, Edward King took Susie's hand and looked into her eyes. "Will you marry me?" he asked.

Susie smiled and tilted her head. She thought about how much she liked this man. He was kind, considerate, and courteous—not just to her, but to everyone. She decided she could make a good life with him.

"Yes, Edward," said Susie. "I'll marry you." Sergeant King shouted for joy. Soon, they were married. At fifteen, Susie was a bride.

When Company E was transferred to Beaufort, South Carolina, Susie went with them. She didn't want to be separated from Edward, so she signed up to work as laundress. However, she had little time to do laundry. Susie cared for the wounded soldiers and helped with the cooking. And, she continued to teach. In the evening, if they weren't on duty or walking picket lines, many of the soldiers came to Susie for lessons. They gathered around the campfire and tried to copy the letters Susie put before them. Their eyes squinted as they tried to read by fire light. They scratched their

necks and slapped at mosquitoes as they put
together letters and sounds to make words.

Unfortunately, many of the men who struggled
to read by fire light, soon struggled for their lives in
the hospital tents.

> *"The sight of several stretchers, each with
> its legless, armless, or desperately wounded
> occupant, entering my ward, admonished me that
> I was there to work, not to wonder or weep. . . ."*
> Louisa May Alcott

# Chapter 5
# Susie the Nurse
## 1863–1865

T he men had waited weeks to fight the Rebels. They planned missions to destroy bridges, roads, and weapons depots important to the Confederate army. Then, in January of 1863, the long wait was over.

"Be careful," Susie warned, hugging Edward tightly.

He gave her a kiss. "Don't you worry, Susie. We can take care of those Rebs." He grinned and picked up his pack and gun. Proudly, Edward and the soldiers from Company E boarded the boats that would take them behind enemy lines.

"Keep safe, Eddie," Susie whispered, as she watched him step aboard.

To keep her mind off Edward, Susie kept busy at the hospital tent. Several men were sick with dysentery and other illnesses caused by crowded camp conditions. She read to them and made them special treats to eat. Susie did all she could to make them comfortable.

"Mrs. King, why you so kind to us?" asked a young soldier. He lay on a cot with a bulky bandage on his foot. "You treat us just like the boys in yo' own Company E."

Susie smiled. "You boys are all the same to me. You're all fighting for our freedom."

"You took an interest in us boys ever since we been here," said another soldier. Susie wiped his brow with a cool cloth. He closed his eyes and sighed with pleasure. "We 'preciate it." Susie rested her hand on his thick, woolly hair. "You boys are welcome."

A few days later, the wounded began to pour in. The hospital tents were full. Even the base hospital at Beaufort was full. Susie worked both sites. She'd catch a ride on the commissary wagon into Beaufort every two or three days and work at the hospital. Then, she'd catch a ride back into camp and work in the hospital tents.

Men lay groaning on cots. Susie spooned medicine into their mouths to help ease the pain. One of the soldiers clutched her hand and cried, "I'm dyin', Miz King. I'm dyin'." He had been shot in the belly; his wound was badly infected. Susie sat with him, holding his hand.

A hospital orderly saw how tired Susie looked. "Get some rest, Miz King," he advised. "You gonna make yo'self sick."

"I don't want to leave him alone," said Susie. She sat with the soldier a long time. Hours later, his fingers loosened their grip and his hand fell back onto the bed. Tears slipped down Susie's face. This man had died fighting for freedom.

Many men died and many more were wounded. As Susie feared, even her own Edward was injured during one of the military expeditions. He fell and hurt his hip while capturing a Rebel soldier. However, it wasn't a severe injury. Susie soon nursed him back to health.

Weeks and months passed. The hospital beds remained full as the fighting continued. Susie kept working. Instead of turning away when she saw men with arms or legs missing, she ran to help. She washed away the blood and dirt and applied fresh, clean, bandages. She bathed their hot, sweaty bodies to reduce fever. She offered cool water to men with dry mouths and parched lips. She helped to feed those who could no longer feed themselves. Wherever a nurse was needed, that's where Susie was.

One day, while working at the base hospital in Beaufort, Susie was introduced to Clara Barton. Mrs. Barton was helping organize nurses for the war effort. Later, she founded the American Red Cross.

"Mrs. Barton," said the quartermaster's wife as she pointed Susie out, "this is one of the best nurses we have in our regiment."

"But . . . she's just a young girl!" exclaimed Mrs. Barton when she saw Susie.

"I'm 16, Ma'am," said Susie.

Together, they walked around the hospital. They chatted with patients and changed bandages. Susie was surprised that such an important person would be interested in her. However, whenever Clara Barton visited Beaufort after that, she made a point to stop in to see Susie. She agreed with the quartermaster's wife—Susie was an excellent nurse.

> *"After the war, a man came along on a red horse; he was dressed in a blue uniform and told us we was free."*
> Adeline Jackson

# Chapter 6
# Mustered Out
## 1865–1866

I n 1865, after four long years, the Civil War finally came to an end. The issue of slavery had been settled. Black people were free.

In a special mustering-out ceremony, Susie and Edward were officially discharged from the army. The men of the regiment stood at attention in cleaned and pressed uniforms. With a loud, clear voice, their commanding officer spoke:

"Nothing can take away the pride we feel, when we look upon the history of . . . the first Black regiment that ever bore arms in defense of freedom on the continent of America," said Colonel Trowbridge.
". . . You have done your duty . . . you have won your freedom. . . ." He told them he was proud to be the leader of such a brave group of

men. Then, he added, "Officers and soldiers of the 33d U.S. Colored Troops . . . I bid you all farewell!"

Susie stood with the men of the 33d. She had left Georgia as a girl. Now, she was a young wife. She had worked long and hard as a teacher and nurse with these men. The war was over. What would she do now?

"I want to stay in Georgia," said Susie.

"I do, too," said Edward. "The South is my home. I don't want to go North like so many other folks."

Susie and Edward moved to Savannah to start their new life. There, they found Grandmother Dolly. She still lived in the old house. Her hair was grayer, her face more wrinkled, and she looked a lot thinner. Susie wrapped her arms around the frail body and breathed in the familiar scent of Grandmother's hair. Everything was just as she had remembered: comfortable, old, cozy.

Edward stood at the door watching the reunion. Susie took his hand and pulled him into the room. "Grandmother," she said, "I'd like you to meet my husband."

Susie and Edward rented a small house not far from Grandmother. Susie got the house ready and made plans to open a school. Edward looked for a job. No one would hire him.

"We don't need a carpenter," some folks said.

"We don't want a Negro carpenter," said others.

"No. No. No," Edward heard almost everywhere he went. Finally, he found a job as a longshoreman, loading and unloading ships.

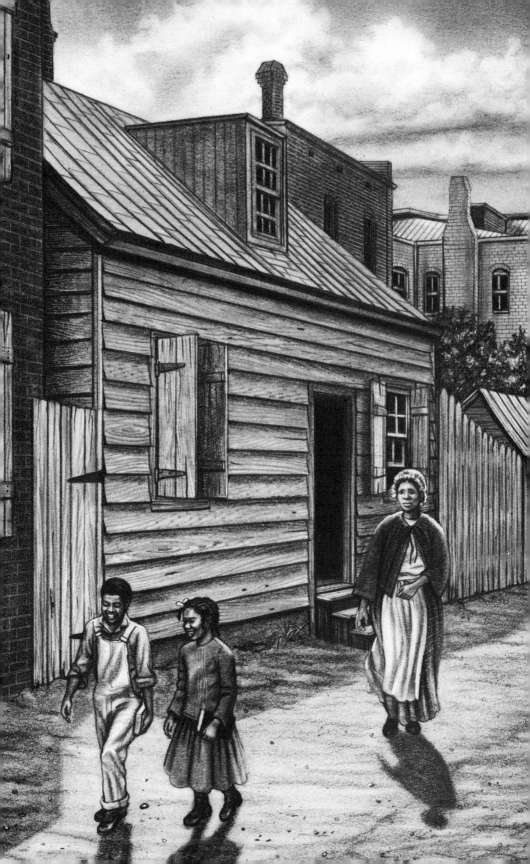

"I thought things would change after the war," he told Susie angrily. "I thought things would be easier for our people."

"The White folks are mad about losing the war," said Susie. "It'll take some time." She rubbed her rounded belly. "But things will be different for our baby."

Edward smiled and kissed Susie gently. "You're right," he agreed. "Things will be different for my son."

While Edward worked on the docks during the day, Susie taught school. She had twenty pupils and charged them each one dollar a month. For several months, Susie and Edward worked hard, saving money and planning for the baby.

On September 16, 1866, there was a loud banging on the front door. One of the men who worked with Edward was standing on the porch. Sweat trickled down his face and he was gasping for breath. "It's Edward, Mrs. King."

Susie was frantic. "What's wrong?"

"He fell. He hit his head . . . bad." He paused, then went on. "I'm afraid he's dead, Ma'am."

"No!" Susie screamed in protest. "Not Edward. Not my Eddie!"

Friends had to help Susie to bed. Grandmother came; she put her arms around Susie and patted her softly.

"It's not fair," Susie cried.

"I know," murmured Grandmother.

"It's not fair," Susie repeated. "He fought all those battles and he was fine. He was safe. And now . . ." she lifted her tear-stained face to

Grandmother, "he's gone." Susie laid her head on Grandmother's breast and sobbed.

Three months later, Susie's baby was born. It was a boy. The son she and Edward had planned for, had come. But, Susie would have to raise him alone.

Susie King Taylor.

> *"I look around now and see the comforts that our younger generation enjoy and think of the blood that was shed to make these comforts possible . . . Let them remember that it was through the efforts of these veterans that . . . we . . . enjoy our liberty today."*
> Susie King Taylor

# Chapter 7
# Pressing On
## 1866–1912

**A**fter the birth of her son in December of 1866, Susie had to close her school—but this was only to be while she regained her strength and took care of her baby. When Susie was ready to start teaching again, she discovered that she had no pupils.

"We're going to the public school now, Mrs. King," said a former student. "And we don't have to pay nothing there."

"My mamma goes to school, too," chipped in another child. "She goes at night and she gets to go for free."

Several public schools for Black children had opened. Many offered free night classes for adults. Susie could no longer earn money as a teacher.

A career in nursing was also closed to her. Even after the war, Black women were not allowed to work in hospitals as nurses. After a long and tiring search, Susie took a job as a maid and cook.

For several years, Susie worked as a maid in the South. Then, she decided to move.

"The Yankee soldiers always talked about Boston," Susie told Grandmother. "They said it was a wonderful place. I think it's time I found out for myself." She hugged Grandmother Dolly goodbye, packed up her son, and headed for Boston.

But, even in Boston, job opportunities were limited. Once more, she found herself working as a maid, cook, or laundress.

In 1879, Susie fell in love again. She married a man named Russell Taylor. Thirteen years after the death of Edward King, Susie was finally able to quit her job and spend time making a home for her son and new husband.

Susie remained concerned about people and the world around her. She never lost interest in her Union "boys in blue." In 1886, she organized a group of volunteers called Corps 67, Women's Relief Corp. They helped the aging veterans and their families.

"Several people in the Women's Relief Corp asked me to write the story of my life," Susie told a friend. "I wasn't too sure about that. I didn't think anyone would be interested!"

"I wrote to our old regiment commander, Colonel Trowbridge, to see what he thought. He said, 'Go ahead! It's just the thing to do.'"

Susie's book was published in 1902.

Susie continued to work for her causes. On October 6, 1912, at the age of 64, Susie died. A small funeral service was held. She was buried quietly in Mount Hope Cemetery in Boston.

Her funeral was not an important event. There were no speeches from city officials. There were no news reporters. There were not many people there at all. But then, they didn't really know who they were burying.

They didn't know that this was Susie Baker, runaway slave. Susie Baker who had started an island school and taught many people to read and write.

They didn't know she was Mrs. Susie King, the first Black Civil War nurse. And one of a few Black women to write about that experience.

They didn't know she was Susie King Taylor, organizer of Corps 67, Womens' Relief Corps.

But we know Susie King Taylor. We know that she made a place in history for herself as a courageous Black woman.

# References

1. Booker, Simeon. (1969). *Susie King Taylor: Civil War Nurse*. New York, NY: McGraw-Hill.

2. Hurmence, Belinda. (1990) *Before Freedom: 48 Oral Histories of Former North and South Carolina Slaves*. New York, NY: Mentor Books, The Penguin Group.

3. McCarthy, Agnes and Lawrence Reddick. (1965). *Worth Fighting For*. New York, NY: Zenith Books, Doubleday and Company.

4. Straubing, Harold Elk. (1993). *In Hospital and Camp: The Civil War Through the Eyes of Its Doctors and Nurses*. Harrisburg, PA: Stackpole Books.

5. Taylor, Susie King. (1968). *Reminiscences of My Life in Camp*. New York, NY: Arno Press and *The New York Times*.

# Bibliography

Biel, Timothy Levi. (1991). *The Civil War.* San Diego, CA: Lucent Books.

Booker, Simeon. (1970). "Susie King Taylor: Teenage Civil War Nurse." *Ebony Magazine*, 25 (4): p. 96–98, 100, 102.

Booker, Simeon. (1969). *Susie King Taylor: Civil War Nurse.* New York, NY: McGraw-Hill.

Dannett, Sylvia G.L. (1964). *Profiles of Negro Womanhood, Vol. 1, 1619–1900.* Yonkers, NY: Educational Heritage, Inc..

Hansen, Joyce. (1993). *Between Two Fires: Black Soldiers in the Civil War.* New York, NY: Franklin Watts.

Hurmence, Belinda. (1990). *Before Freedom: 48 Oral Histories of Former North and South Carolina Slaves.* New York, NY: Mentor Books, the Penguin Group.

Mainiero, Lina. *American Women Writers From Colonial Times to Present. A Critical Reference Guide. Vol. 4, S–Z.* New York, NY: Frederick Ungar Publishing Co.

McCarthy, Agnes and Lawrence Reddick. (1965). *Worth Fighting For.* New York, NY: Zenith Books, Doubleday and Company, Inc.

Reeder, Colonel Red. (1966). *The Story of the Civil War.* Eau Claire, IN: E.M. Hale and Company.

Smith, Jesse Carney. *Notable Black American Women.* Detroit, MI: Gale Research Inc.

Straubing, Harold Elk. (1993). *In Hospital and Camp: The Civil War Through the Eyes of Its Doctors and Nurses.* Harrisburg, PA: Stackpole Books.

Taylor, Susie King. (1968). *Reminiscences of My Life In Camp.* New York, NY: Arno Press and *The New York Times.*

Taylor, Susie King. (1988). *A Black Woman's Civil War Memoirs.* Edited by Romero, Patricia. Princeton, NJ: Markus Wiener Publishing, Inc.

# Suggested Reading

Cornish, Dudley Taylor. (1987). *The Sable Arm: Black Troops in the Union Army, 1861–1865.* Kansas City, KS:University Press of Kansas.

Gooding, James Henry. (1991). *On the Alter of Freedom: A Black Soldier's Civil War Letters From the Front.* Amherst, MA: University of Massachusetts Press.

Hansen, Joyce. (1993). *Between Two Fires: Black Soldiers in the Civil War.* New York, NY: Franklin Watts.

## About the Author

Denise M. Jordan has had numerous articles published, but *Susie King Taylor: Destined to Be Free* is her first children's book. She attended Indiana University School of Nursing and currently teaches nursing at Ivy Tech State College. Ms. Jordan, her husband Willie, and their three children live in Fort Wayne, Indiana.

## About the Illustrator

Higgins Bond began painting when she was twelve, but her career as an artist began as a student at Memphis College of Art. Since then, she has illustrated numerous book jackets and record albums—in addition to the portraits of Jan Matzeliger and W.E.B. DuBois for the United States Postal Service's "Black Heritage" stamp series. Her first children's book, *When I Was Little*, is currently available through Just Us Books. She lives in New Jersey with her husband and son.